KING of the DOGS

by Jacqueline Adams

Table of Contents

A Brave Leader in a Cold Land

It was February 1911, and Captain Robert Scott was on a dangerous expedition across the frozen Antarctic wilderness. Every day, his two teams of dogs pulled heavy sleds packed with supplies many miles across the ice and snow.

Scott's dogs were from Siberia, Russia, where they had pulled sleds piled with mail through long, freezing winters. Because they had survived in icy Siberia, Scott knew that his dogs were strong, tough, and courageous.

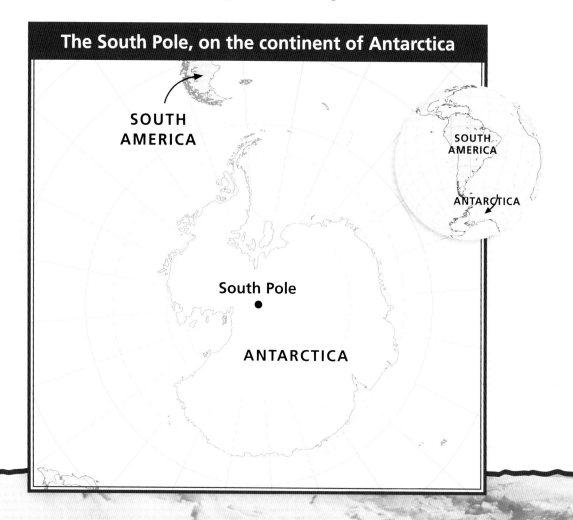

The South Pole, on the continent of Antarctica

SOUTH AMERICA

SOUTH AMERICA

ANTARCTICA

South Pole

ANTARCTICA

Scott needed dogs he could count on to help him
achieve his dream: to be the first person to reach the
South Pole. He was exploring Antarctica now to prepare
for that future journey, and setting up depots (DEE-pohz),
places where supplies are stored. The following year he
planned to camp near those depots on his way to the
South Pole. Without strong dogs to pull the heavy sleds,
he would not be able to stockpile enough supplies for his
next trip.

One dog stood out from all the others. That dog
was Osman. He was big and had dark, thick, shaggy fur.
He looked wild, more like a wolf than a dog. His ears
pointed forward and his eyes shone brightly, making him
look as if he was ready for anything. One of Scott's men
called Osman the "king-dog."

Scott had three other men with him on this trip, two scientists and an expert in handling sled dogs. None of the men knew how truly remarkable Osman was until they had started the journey.

Scott had chosen Osman to be the leader of one of the two dog teams. That meant he always ran in front of the other dogs. The twelve other dogs on Osman's team lined up in pairs behind him.

Each dog wore a strap called a harness. Scott attached all the harnesses to a rope, and then attached the rope to a big, heavy sled loaded with supplies. The dogs had to work extremely hard to pull it, and they often grew tired. On the first three days of the journey, they ran about 78 miles (125 kilometers) each day. But after they had rested, the dogs were always anxious to get going again.

The dog teams pulled heavy sleds loaded with food, dog food, fuel, sleeping bags, tents, cooking tools, and other equipment. Survival in the coldest place in the world depended on being well prepared.

Danger in the Snow

February 21 was cold and gray. Osman's team took off around ten o'clock in the evening, the sled's runners flying over the crusty snow. Sometimes a freezing wind blasted the dogs and made the air even colder, but that night the wind was still.

Wind and cold were not the most dangerous things on the expedition. The real danger lurked under the snow. Scott's men knew that thick ice sheets covered much of Antarctica, and that huge cracks, or crevasses, sometimes opened in the ice. Snow and the dim light made it hard for the men to spot these crevasses as they moved ahead with the sleds.

That night, the dogs began to get tired. They were breathing hard as they raced across the ice. Then Scott and his men began to see the outlines of some crevasses in the snow. They knew they were in a dangerous area, but it was too late to change course. Scott had been running next to the sled, but now he hopped on.

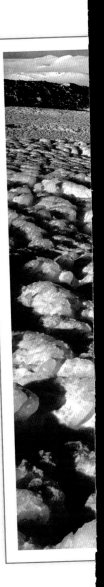

Some Antarctic crevasses can be as deep as 300 feet (91 meters). That's as deep as a soccer field is long.

Polar Extremes

Antarctica is south of the equator, on the very bottom of a world map or globe. Summer in Antarctica is from December 21 to March 21. The summer months have 24 hours of daylight! This allowed Scott's expedition to travel at night.

A Terrible Accident

Suddenly, two dogs on Osman's team disappeared, sinking down through the ice and snow. Then, two by two, they all began to vanish. The entire team was falling into a huge, hidden crevasse.

Only Osman was left. He struggled to keep a foothold on one side of the crevasse, while the sled sat on the other side. The other dogs on Osman's team dangled in midair in their harnesses inside the icy crevasse. Empty space stretched below them. Scott and his partner rushed to the edge of the crevasse and peered down—the dogs were howling, badly frightened.

Scott knew that if Osman couldn't hold on, all the dogs would fall—and pull the sled down with them. The whole team of dogs would be lost, along with all of the supplies strapped to the sled.

The rope between the dogs and Osman cut into the soft snow. It dug into the side of the crevasse, and the men couldn't lift it. They couldn't move the rope attached to the sled, either. It bit deeply into the snow on the other side of the crevasse.

Osman dug his claws deeper into the ice. The twelve dogs were so heavy. Their enormous weight, probably about 600 pounds (272 kilograms) pulled Osman's harness too tightly. The harness was choking him, and he could barely breathe.

At first, Captain Scott feared that he would not be able to save Osman and the other dogs on his team.

Saving Osman

Minutes went by as Osman struggled to keep the other dogs from pulling him into the crevasse. He needed all of his strength to hold on, and he was quickly tiring.

Then Scott came up with a plan. First he laid tent poles across the crevasse, which was about 5 feet (1.5 meters) wide. Then he very carefully lay down on top of the poles. In his hand, he had a short rope from one of the sleeping bags. He reached down and tied it to the main rope that was holding the dangling dogs.

The men from the other sled had come to help. One of them jumped over a narrow part of the crevasse. He grabbed the short rope and pulled up on it. It lifted the main rope, which was still dug into the ground, a few inches. This loosened the rope pulling on Osman's harness and stopped him from choking.

Scott's men worked as a team to help carry out his plan to rescue the dogs.

Scott's men took the main dog rope that was attached to Osman's harness and tied it to a stake. Then they drove the stake into the ground, so the rope wouldn't slip away. They did the same thing with the other end of the rope, which was attached to the sled. The dog team was safe for the moment.

Osman gasped for air as the men cut his harness. He was free, but the other dogs were still in danger. Osman had done all he could to save his team—now it was time for the men to do the rest.

Amazing Antarctica

Antarctica is the coldest place on Earth. In some places, the temperature can fall to below −80°F (−62°C) in winter. But it can get up to 50°F (10°C) along the coast in summer.

About 98% of Antarctica is covered by an ice sheet that in some places is about 2.5 miles (4 kilometers) deep. Snowfall over hundreds of thousands of years created the ice sheet, which is shaped like a dome. Under the ice lies another world—of valleys, mountains, and plains.

Siberian huskies like Osman have long, thick fur that keeps them from getting frostbitten in the snow and severe cold.

Saving the Other Dogs

The men now turned their attention to the dogs inside the crevasse. Two dogs had fallen out of their harnesses, landing on a snowy ledge far below—about 65 feet (20 meters) down. For now, they were resting and seemed safe.

But the other ten dogs were in trouble. They were still attached to the main rope, hanging in the air with their harnesses digging into them. The terrified dogs howled and cried and twisted around, trying to escape from the harnesses.

The men went to work, sliding the sled onto the tent poles that still crossed the crevasse. The sled was now a bridge that the men could stand on. They used the main rope to pull the dogs up to the sled, two by two, and cut each one out of its harness.

Only the two fallen dogs on the ledge were left. Scott refused to leave them there to die. He had an idea to save them. At least one of his men thought it was dangerous, but Scott didn't care.

The Distance

How far down into the crevasse was 65 feet (20 meters)? That's about the height of a six-story building!

Captain Scott refused to leave the dogs on the ledge.

The men used a strong rope to lower Scott down the 65 feet into the crevasse. The frightened dogs were happy to see him. Scott stood on the ledge while the men pulled up each dog, one at a time, still attached to the main rope. Once both dogs were safe, Scott came up, too.

The men and the dogs were very tired, their bodies in pain from all the pulling and struggling. The rescue had taken two-and-a-half hours.

Later that night, Scott and his men rested in their tent. The dogs rested outside. One thing was clear: Scott had made the right choice when he picked Osman to lead his dog team. Without the lead dog's strength and courage, the other twelve animals would have fallen to the bottom of the crevasse. Rescuing them would have been impossible. The dogs were safe, thanks to their king, Osman.

End Note

Osman survived the dangerous journey in Antarctica. He later enjoyed a happy retirement in New Zealand.